PERFECTLY DRESSED *Salads*

PERFECTLY *Salads*
DRESSED

60 delicious dressing recipes from tangy vinaigrettes to creamy mayos

RYLAND PETERS & SMALL
LONDON • NEW YORK

Senior Designer Toni Kay
Head of Production Patricia Harrington
Art Director Leslie Harrington
Editorial Director Julia Charles
Publisher Cindy Richards
Food and Prop Styling Louise Pickford
Indexer Hilary Bird

First published in 2014. This updated
and extended edition published in
2021 by Ryland Peters & Small
20–21 Jockey's Fields
London WC1R 4BW
and
341 E 116th Street
New York, 10029

www.rylandpeters.com

10 9 8 7 6 5 4 3 2 1

Text © Louise Pickford 2014, 2021
with the exception of recipes
credited on page 96. Design and
photographs © Ryland Peters &
Small 2014, 2021.

Printed in China

ISBN: 978-1-78879-359-9

A CIP record for this book is
available from the British Library.

US Library of Congress CIP data
has been applied for.

NOTES
• Both metric and imperial oz./
US cups are included. Work with one
set of measurements and do not
alternate between the two within
a recipe. All spoon measurements
given are level:
1 teaspoon = 5 ml;
1 tablespoon = 15 ml.
• Uncooked or partially cooked eggs
should not be served to the elderly
or frail, young children, pregnant
women or those with compromised
immune systems.
• When a recipe calls for citrus zest
or peel, buy unwaxed fruit and wash
well before using. If you can only
find treated fruit, scrub well in
warm soapy water before using.
• To sterilize screw-top jars and
bottles for storing dressings,
preheat the oven to 150°C
fan/160°C/325°F/ Gas 3. Wash
the jars and/or bottles and their
lids in hot soapy water then rinse
but don't dry them. Remove any
rubber seals, put the jars onto a
baking sheet and into the oven for
10 minutes. Soak the lids in boiling
water for a few minutes.

Contents

Introduction

A salad without a dressing would be no salad at all. Of course there are as many dressings as salads so compiling this collection was, much like a dressing itself, a balancing act to ensure I managed to cover as many different types of dressings as I could.

Dressings can be divided into two main categories; vinaigrettes (an oil and vinegar dressing lightly whisked together until amalgamated just prior to use) and creamy dressings or emulsions (where oil and vinegar are whisked with another element until thickened permanently). These make up two chapters in this book whilst a further four chapters – fruity, herbed, infused and warm dressings – cover variations of these.

So what is vinaigrette? The word derives from the French 'vinaigre' or 'sour wine'. A vinaigrette generally consists of three parts oil to one part vinegar or citrus (although this will vary according to taste) and can be made using various oils such as olive, walnut, hazelnut, sunflower and grape seed oil. Vinegars, too, vary greatly and include white and red wine vinegar, raspberry and other fruit vinegars, cider and balsamic vinegar.

Creamy dressings are a mixture of oil and vinegar that require the addition of an emulsifier in order to remain permanently stable. Emulsifying agents include egg and mustard and go to make such classic dressings as mayonnaise and Caesar salad dressing. Again, creamy dressings can be flavoured with various other elements ranging from ketchup and Worcestershire sauce, to fresh herbs and spices, as well as finely chopped shallots.

In the fruity dressings section I have included fruit-based vinegars as well as puréed fruits such as mango, a homemade pomegranate syrup and even diced fresh peach dressing. Herbed dressings are flavoured with finely chopped herbs added to a simple oil and vinegar mixture along with cream, mayonnaise or yogurt, with additional flavours such as horseradish.

Infused dressings differ slightly as the oil is infused first with herbs, spices or citrus, strained and then blended with vinegar. This gives the oil and subsequently the dressing its underlying flavour and characteristic. Warm (or cooked) dressings are where the integral ingredients are first heated in a pan to cook them and then vinegar (or citrus juice) and oil are added, the resulting dressing is then poured warm over the salad.

Once made, dressings should be used as soon as possible – if you do make a vinaigrette ahead of time, be sure to blend again just prior to serving. If you are storing any dressings, keep them in a sealed container in the fridge for 2–3 days. Return to room temperature before using and shake well if needed.

The serving suggestions I give in each recipe are a guideline only and you can enjoy each dressing with any salad you like. As you will discover over the following pages there is a simply staggering amount of wonderful and different dressings, which of course means a equally staggering amount of delicious salads.

VINAIGRETTES

Tarragon • Champagne vinegar • Sweet chilli • Mild Curry •
Japanese-style sweet miso and sesame • Wasabi, lemon and avocado oil •
Wafu • Szechuan chilli • Chilli and sesame • Lemon and coriander •
Bloody Mary • Smoky barbecue • Walnut and vincotto • Hazelnut •
Reduced balsamic • French • Mustard

Tarragon

When available, use macadamia nut oil in this dressing as it has a lovely mild nutty flavour that really shows off the tarragon to its best. Hazelnut oil is also good and perhaps a more readily available alternative. If you love the flavour of tarragon, use tarragon vinegar.

2 teaspoons white wine or tarragon vinegar
1 teaspoon Dijon mustard
1/2–1 teaspoon caster/granulated sugar
2 tablespoons freshly chopped tarragon
3 tablespoons macadamia or hazelnut oil
1 tablespoon extra virgin olive oil
salt and freshly ground black pepper

MAKES 125 ML/1/2 CUP

Place the vinegar, mustard, sugar, tarragon and a little salt and pepper in a blender and blend until combined, then add both the oils and blend again until amalgamated. Adjust the seasoning and serve.

This dressing goes beautifully with a poached salmon salad.

Champagne vinegar

Champagne, like wine, can be used to make vinegar and produces a mild vinegar made from dry white sparkling wine. It is available from specialist food stores.

2 tablespoons champagne vinegar
6 tablespoons extra virgin olive oil
salt and freshly ground black pepper

MAKES 125 ML/1/2 CUP

Place the vinegar, oil and some salt and pepper in a screw-top jar, seal and shake well until the dressing is amalgamated. Adjust the seasoning and serve.

This is lovely served with salad leaves, crumbled goat's cheese and very thinly sliced pears.

Sweet chilli

Hot, sweet and sour together is a flavour combination we associate with Far East Asian cuisine and this dressing epitomises that. Using bird's eye chillies/chiles will result in a fiery dressing so, if you prefer a milder heat, either discard the seeds or use 1 large, mild chilli/chile.

75 ml/⅓ cup rice wine vinegar
50 g/¼ cup granulated sugar
2 red bird's eye chillies/chiles, thinly sliced
6 tablespoons peanut oil
freshly squeezed juice of ½ lime
2 tablespoons Thai fish sauce
salt

MAKES 150 ML/⅔ CUP

Place the vinegar, sugar and 1 tablespoon water in a small saucepan and heat gently to dissolve the sugar, then simmer for 5 minutes until the mixture is syrupy. Stir in the sliced chillies/chiles and allow to cool completely.

Whisk in the remaining ingredients until the dressing is amalgamated and adjust the seasoning to taste.

This is wonderful drizzled over a Thai beef salad with tomatoes, cucumber, red onions and fresh herbs.

Mild curry

The curry spices are softened with onion, garlic and ginger and then strained so that the resulting oil has a deep curry flavour without the bits. The oil is then whisked with lemon and a little cream, making a wonderfully aromatic dressing.

3 tablespoons sunflower oil
1 small onion, finely chopped
1 garlic clove, crushed
1 teaspoon grated root ginger
1 teaspoon curry powder
2 teaspoons freshly squeezed lemon juice
3 tablespoons extra virgin olive oil
1 tablespoon single/light cream
salt and freshly ground black pepper

MAKES 125 ML/½ CUP

Heat the sunflower oil in a small frying pan/skillet and gently fry the onion, garlic, ginger, curry powder and a little salt and pepper over a low heat for 5 minutes until softened. Strain the mixture through a fine-mesh sieve/strainer and set aside to cool.

Stir in the lemon juice and then whisk in the olive oil and cream until smooth and amalgamated. Adjust seasoning to taste.

Serve this with a shredded chicken, celery and walnut salad.

Thai beef salad with
Sweet chilli dressing

Japanese-style sweet miso and sesame

Miso paste, made from fermented soya beans, is used extensively in Japanese cooking. It is salty, earthy and malty and adds a rich depth of flavour to dishes. Here it is sweetened and combined with sesame oil. You can buy miso paste from Asian stores, health food stores or larger supermarkets – there are several types available but any can be used in this dressing.

2 tablespoons sunflower oil
2 tablespoons rice wine vinegar
2 tablespoons miso paste
2 teaspoons caster/granulated sugar
2 teaspoons sesame oil

MAKES 125 ML/½ CUP

Place all the ingredients in a screw-top jar and shake well until evenly blended. If the sauce is a little thick, thin slightly by whisking in a teaspoon of water.

This robust dressing is perfect tossed with cooked noodles, shredded vegetables and topped with toasted sesame seeds.

Wasabi, lemon and avocado oil

Wasabi is Japanese horseradish, an integral ingredient in sushi and an accompaniment to sashimi. It adds a wonderful pungency to dishes and is lovely in a salad dressing. Rather than combining it with other traditional Japanese ingredients, here it is whisked with avocado oil and lemon juice for a refreshingly different dressing.

1 teaspoon wasabi paste
½ teaspoon caster/granulated sugar
1 tablespoon freshly squeezed
   lemon or lime juice
3 tablespoons avocado oil
a pinch of salt

MAKES 75 ML/⅓ CUP

Place the wasabi paste, sugar, lemon or lime juice and a pinch of salt in a bowl and, using a small balloon whisk, blend to form a smooth paste. Gradually whisk in the oil until amalgamated and adjust the seasoning to taste.

This is delicious drizzled over raw tuna or beef carpaccio or a cooked prawn/shrimp salad.

Wafu

Literally translated as 'Japanese-style', wafu is a soy, vinegar and sesame dressing to which other flavourings can be added. It is a great recipe to have in your culinary arsenal.

1 small shallot, very finely chopped
2 tablespoons Japanese soy sauce
2 tablespoons rice wine vinegar
2 tablespoons dashi broth
2 teaspoons sesame oil
2 teaspoons caster/granulated sugar
1 teaspoon freshly grated ginger
1/2 teaspoon crushed garlic

MAKES 150 ML/2/3 CUP

Put all the ingredients in a screw-top glass jar, screw the lid on tightly and shake well until amalgamated.

Delicious drizzled over simple leaf salads or more complex noodle salads.

Szechuan chilli

Perfect for dipping steamed and fried wontons into or drizzling over noodle and shredded vegetable salads.

100 ml/1/3 cup sunflower oil
1–2 teaspoons dried red chilli/hot red pepper flakes
2 tablespoons light soy sauce
1 tablespoon black vinegar
2 teaspoons caster/granulated sugar
1/4 teaspoon Szechuan peppercorns

MAKES 150 ML/2/3 CUP

Heat the oil in a small saucepan set over a medium heat until it just starts to shimmer. Remove from the heat and stir in the chilli/hot red pepper flakes. Set aside for 30 minutes, then strain through a fine-mesh sieve/strainer into a clean bowl. Stir in the remaining ingredients and serve as required.

TIP If you are making this dressing ahead of time, omit the peppercorns and add just before serving.

Chilli and sesame

The base of this dressing is a sweet and savoury syrup made with sugar and rice wine vinegar. The remaining ingredients are then whisked into the cooled syrup. You can use sunflower oil instead of peanut oil if preferred.

2 teaspoons caster/granulated sugar
1 tablespoon rice wine vinegar
1/4 teaspoon salt
1 tablespoon light soy sauce
2–3 tablespoons peanut oil
1–2 teaspoons toasted sesame oil
1 large red chilli/chile, seeded and finely chopped

MAKES 150 ML/²/₃ CUP

Place the sugar, vinegar and salt in a small saucepan with 1 tablespoon of cold water. Heat gently until the sugar dissolves, then increase the heat and simmer for 2 minutes. Remove from the heat and allow to go cold.

Place the cooled mixture in a screw-top jar with the remaining ingredients, seal the lid and shake well until evenly blended. Adjust the seasoning and serve.

This is fab with a Chinese-style shredded rice noodle, vegetable and tofu salad.

Lemon and coriander

Lemon and coriander/cilantro are perfect partners in this fresh-tasting dressing, with a hint of nuttiness provided by the two oils.

5 tablespoons/¹/₃ cup peanut oil
1 tablespoon toasted sesame oil
freshly squeezed juice of 1 lemon
2 tablespoons sweet soy sauce (Indonesian ketchap manis), or regular soy sauce with 1/2 teaspoon sugar added
2 tablespoons freshly chopped coriander/cilantro
1 garlic clove, crushed
freshly ground black pepper

MAKES 150 ML/²/₃ CUP

Put the ingredients in a screw-top jar, shake well and adjust the black pepper to taste. If storing in the fridge, omit the coriander/cilantro and add just before use.

This dressing goes very well with a salad of char-grilled squid and spinach leaves.

Noodle and tofu salad with
Chilli and sesame dressing

Freshly-shucked oysters
with *Bloody Mary dressing*

Bloody Mary

Using a ripe tomato rather than tomato juice in this dressing version of the classic 'morning after' pick-me- up adds a lovely refreshing tang to it.

1 ripe tomato, roughly chopped
1 tablespoon vodka
2 teaspoons white wine vinegar
1 teaspoon Worcestershire sauce
a few drops of Tabasco
a pinch of celery salt
2 tablespoons extra virgin olive oil
freshly ground black pepper
freshly squeezed lemon juice, to taste

MAKES 125 ML/½ CUP

Place the tomato in a blender and add the vodka, white wine vinegar, Worcestershire sauce, Tabasco, celery salt and a little black pepper. Purée until smooth, then transfer to a bowl and gradually whisk in the oil until the dressing is emulsified. Add enough lemon juice for your taste and adjust seasoning.

This is fabulous drizzled over a plate of freshly shucked oysters.

Smoky barbecue

By char-grilling the chilli/chile, garlic and tomato over a gas flame the smoky flavour permeates the flesh, giving this dressing its distinctive flavour.

1 large red chilli/chile
1 large garlic clove
1 tomato
1 tablespoon red wine vinegar
1 teaspoon Dijon mustard
2 teaspoons Worcestershire sauce
2 teaspoons molasses
½ teaspoon smoked paprika
2 tablespoons extra virgin olive oil
salt and freshly ground black pepper

MAKES 200 ML/¾ CUP

Thread the chilli/chile and unpeeled garlic clove onto a metal skewer and char-grill over a gas flame, turning, until evenly charred. Set aside to cool. Using tongs to hold the tomato, char-grill the skin over the flame.

Peel the skin from the chilli/chile, garlic and tomato. De-seed the chilli/chile and finely chop the flesh. Crush the garlic. De-seed and finely dice the tomato flesh.

Place the tomato, chilli/chile, garlic, vinegar, mustard, Worcestershire sauce, molasses, smoked paprika and a little salt and pepper in a blender and purée until really smooth. Transfer to a bowl and whisk in the oil. Adjust the seasoning to taste and serve.

Walnut and vincotto

Vincotto (cooked wine) is a sweet, dark syrup made from fermented grape must and comes from Apulia in the south of Italy. It is available from Italian delis and specialist food stores.

1 tablespoon vincotto
2 teaspoons red wine vinegar
3 tablespoons walnut oil
1 tablespoon extra virgin olive oil
salt and freshly ground black pepper

MAKES 75 ML/⅓ CUP

Whisk all the ingredients together, adjust the seasoning and serve.

Perfect drizzled over a tomato and rocket/arugula salad with shavings of aged Parmesan.

Hazelnut

A lovely simple vinaigrette that is nonetheless delicious. The raspberry vinegar seems to complement the nut oil beautifully.

2 teaspoons raspberry vinegar
1 teaspoon caster/granulated sugar
4 tablespoons hazelnut oil
salt and freshly ground black pepper

MAKES 75 ML/⅓ CUP

Whisk the vinegar, sugar, salt and pepper together and then whisk in the oil until amalgamated. Adjust the seasoning to taste.

Serve with a green leaf salad.

Reduced balsamic

Making your own reduced balsamic vinegar is a great way of transforming an inexpensive vinegar into a fabulous sweet balsamic caramel and consequently a delicious vinaigrette. Just be sure to watch the vinegar closely as it reduces as it will easily go too far and become burnt vinegar!

500 ml/17 fl. oz. bottle of inexpensive balsamic vinegar
5 tablespoons extra virgin olive oil
2 tablespoons reduced balsamic (see method)
salt and freshly ground black pepper

MAKES 100 ML/⅓ CUP PLUS 1 TABLESPOON

Place the balsamic vinegar in a small pan and simmer over a high heat for about 10 minutes until approximately 150 ml/⅔ cup remains and the vinegar is think and syrupy. Allow to cool completely.

Combine the oil, 2 tablespoons of the reduced balsamic vinegar and salt and pepper together, whisking well and serve. (The remaining reduced balsamic vinegar can be stored in a screw-top jar.)

This versatile dressing works well on green leaves, any type of tomato salad and is, of course, perfect with a Caprese salad of tomatoes, avocado and mozzarella.

French

Today the term French dressing is universal, but originally it was used to describe a vinaigrette. It is an emulsion of oil and vinegar in varying quantities and any type of oil can be used along with an acid of either vinegar or citrus juice. To make a really good French dressing the balance of flavours should be just right – neither too sharp, or too oily – and, once made, it will keep well for several days in a screw-top jar in the fridge. Shake well before using.

1 tablespoon Chardonnay
  white wine vinegar
1 teaspoon Dijon mustard
a pinch of sugar
4 tablespoons extra virgin olive oil
2 tablespoons sunflower oil
salt and freshly ground black pepper

**MAKES 100 ML/⅓ CUP
PLUS 1 TABLESPOON**

In a bowl stir together the vinegar, mustard, sugar, salt and pepper until smooth and then gradually whisk in the oils until amalgamated. Season to taste and serve.

Use on any salad of your choice.

Mustard

Here Dijon mustard and whole grain mustard are used together to give the resulting dressing both a creamy and grainy texture which is lovely on a salad of crisp leaves.

1½ teaspoons Dijon mustard
1½ teaspoons whole grain mustard
2 teaspoons red wine vinegar
a pinch of caster/granulated sugar
4 tablespoons extra virgin olive oil
salt and freshly ground black pepper

MAKES 100 ML/⅓ CUP
PLUS 1 TABLESPOON

Place the two mustards, the vinegar, sugar and a little salt and pepper in a bowl and stir well until smooth. Gradually whisk in the oil until the dressing is amalgamated, adjust seasoning and serve.

VARIATION
For tarragon mustard dressing add 1 tablespoon freshly chopped tarragon to the finished oil.

CREAMY DRESSINGS

Mayonnaise • Ranch • Alioli • Vegan tofu alioli • Green goddess • Caesar •
Blue cheese • Goat's cheese and basil • Herbed labne • Creamy Russian •
Avocado and tarragon • Coconut and chilli • Louis • Marie rose

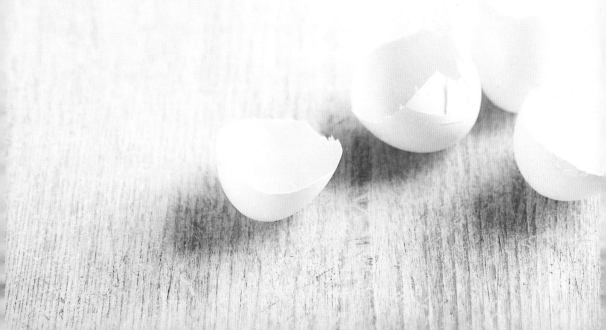

Mayonnaise

In order to make mayonnaise, you must form a permanent emulsion of two ingredients that ordinarily do not mix together, in this case egg yolks and oil. Using half extra virgin olive oil and half pure olive oil produces a milder flavour.

3 egg yolks
2 teaspoons white wine vinegar or
    freshly squeezed lemon juice
1 teaspoon Dijon mustard
150 ml/²/₃ cup fruity extra virgin olive oil
150 ml/²/₃ cup olive oil
salt and ground white pepper

MAKES 300 ML/1¼ CUPS

Place the egg yolks, vinegar, mustard and a little salt and pepper in a bowl and, using electric beaters, whisk until the mixture is frothy. Then very gradually whisk in the two oils, a little at a time, whisking well after each addition until the sauce is thickened and glossy and all the oil incorporated. If the mixture is too thick, thin it with a teaspoon or so of boiling water until you reach the required consistency.

Adjust the seasoning to taste and serve.

VARIATION
Wasabi – stir 1 tablespoon wasabi paste and 2 tablespoons rice wine vinegar into the basic mayonnaise recipe above.

Ranch

Named after the Dude Ranch run by Steve Henson and his wife Gail in California in the 1950s, after they invented a creamy, lightly spiced dressing for the salads they served. It was so popular with guests that they started to make small bottles and a spice mix to take away. Its popularity grew to such an extent that they were shipping it all over the States. Today it is the largest selling dressing in the US - you will find many different brands available in stores, but of course home-made is always the best.

125 ml/½ cup buttermilk
150 g/²/₃ cup mayonnaise (see left)
1 tablespoon freshly chopped chives
1 tablespoon freshly chopped parsley
1 garlic clove, crushed
1 teaspoon mild American mustard
a few drops of Tabasco sauce, optional
salt and freshly ground black pepper

MAKES 200 ML/³/₄ CUP

Whisk all the ingredients together and season to taste.

Serve this as a dressing to go with a grilled chicken salad with Little Gem/Boston lettuce.

Alioli

Add more or less garlic depending on what you prefer - either way it will be delicious!

3 egg yolks
2–4 garlic cloves, crushed
2 teaspoons white wine vinegar
½ teaspoon Dijon mustard
125 ml/½ cup fruity extra virgin olive oil
125 ml/½ cup olive oil
sea salt and ground white pepper

LEMON ALIOLI
grated zest and freshly squeezed juice
    of ½ lemon

SAFFRON ALIOLI
a pinch of saffron strands
1 tablespoon boiling water

HARISSA ALIOLI
2–3 teaspoons harissa paste

MAKES 300 ML/1¼ CUPS

Place the egg yolks, garlic, vinegar, mustard and a little salt and pepper in a bowl and use electric beaters to whisk/beat until frothy.

In a separate bowl, combine the oils together and gradually add to the yolks a little at a time, beating well after each addition, until the sauce is thickened and glossy and all of the oil is incorporated. It should be able to hold its shape. If the mixture is too thick, thin it with a teaspoon or so of boiling water, until you reach the required consistency.

VARIATIONS
Lemon Alioli Follow the basic recipe above, adding the lemon zest to the egg yolks and replacing the vinegar with the lemon juice.

Saffron Alioli Soak the saffron strands in the boiling water for 5 minutes. In the meantime, follow the basic recipe, then add the saffron strands and the infused water to the alioli and whisk/beat again, until evenly mixed.

Harissa Alioli Follow the basic recipe, then stir in the harissa paste, to taste.

Vegan tofu alioli

No need to miss out on this delicious sauce if you are vegan or egg intolerant with this egg-free version of alioli.

250 g/9 oz. silken tofu, drained
3 tablespoons tahini paste
2 tablespoons extra virgin olive oil
1 garlic clove, crushed
2 tablespoons freshly squeezed lemon juice
sea salt and freshly ground black pepper

SAFFRON TOFU ALIOLI
a small pinch of saffron strands
1 teaspoon boiling water

MAKES 300 ML/1¼ CUPS

Place all the ingredients in a bowl and whisk/beat until smooth.

VARIATION
Saffron Tofu Alioli Soak the saffron strands in the boiling water for 5 minutes. In the meantime, follow the basic recipe above, then add the saffron strands and the infused water to the tofu alioli and whisk/beat again, until evenly mixed.

Green goddess

Invented in the 1920s and named after the famous movie of the time The Green Goddess, this mayonnaise-based dressing is, as the name suggests, tinted green by the inclusion of fresh herbs. It was an adaptation of the French 'sauce vert' and is commonly served with crab-based salads. You can use any combination of fresh herbs you like.

2 tablespoons freshly chopped mixed herbs,
    such as parsley, tarragon and chives
1 white anchovy fillet in oil, drained and chopped
1 spring onion/scallion, trimmed and chopped
1 small garlic clove, crushed
150 g/²/₃ cup mayonnaise (see page 29)
2 tablespoons milk
1 tablespoon white wine vinegar
salt and freshly ground black pepper

MAKES 250 ML/1 CUP PLUS 1 TABLESPOON

Place all the ingredients in a blender and blend until smooth. Adjust the seasoning to taste and serve with a shellfish and lettuce salad.

Caesar

There are endless recipes for both a Caesar salad and its dressing and almost every restaurant serves its own version. To my mind the best dressing always includes egg, garlic, anchovies and grated Parmesan. I like it with a good tang of anchovy but you should use as little or as much as you like.

1 medium egg
1 tablespoon white wine vinegar
2–4 anchovies in oil, drained and chopped
1 garlic clove, crushed
1 teaspoon Worcestershire sauce
125 ml/¹/₂ cup extra virgin olive oil
3 tablespoons freshly grated Parmesan
salt and pepper

MAKES 175 ML/SCANT ³/₄ CUP

Boil the egg in a saucepan of water for 3 minutes, then immediately plunge into cold water. Shell the egg and place in a food processor. Add the vinegar, anchovies, garlic, Worcestershire sauce and a little salt and pepper and blend until frothy. Gradually whisk in the oil in a steady stream until the sauce is thickened. Stir in the cheese and adjust seasoning to taste.

Serve drizzled over a cos lettuce, crouton, anchovy and Parmesan salad – if you like, you can add crispy fried bacon as well.

Blue cheese

A classic dressing for wedges of chilled cos or iceberg lettuce - you can experiment with different types of blue cheese to give you the flavour that works best for you. This recipe uses a creamy St Agur, which has a milder taste than Gorgonzola or Roquefort, but really it's up to you.

75 g/¹/₃ cup sour(ed) cream
50 g/¹/₄ cup creamy blue cheese
1 tablespoon white wine vinegar
2 teaspoons just-boiled water
2 tablespoons extra virgin olive oil
1 tablespoon freshly chopped chives
salt and freshly ground black pepper

MAKES 200 ML/³/₄ CUP

Place the sour(ed) cream, blue cheese, vinegar, water and a little salt and pepper in a blender and whizz until fairly smooth. Add the oil and blend again. Stir in the chives, adjust the seasoning to taste and serve.

This creamy dressing with its lovely tang of acidity from the blue cheese is wonderful with cos or iceberg lettuce. It also works well with all green leaf salads, celery, apple, pear and mixed nuts.

Goat's cheese and basil

A creamy dressing with a tang of goat's cheese makes a delicious foil for a salad of mixed tomatoes. It could also be used as an alternative to the Caesar dressing on page 33.

100 g/scant ¹/₂ cup soft goat's cheese
4 tablespoons runny yogurt
2 tablespoons warm water
2 teaspoons white wine vinegar
1 tablespoon finely chopped basil
salt and freshly ground black pepper

MAKES 200 ML/³/₄ CUP

Place the cheese, yogurt, water and vinegar in a blender and blend until smooth. Add the basil and blend again until the sauce is speckled and a pale green colour. Season to taste and serve.

This dressing is perfect over a medley of different types of tomatoes, pitted/stoned black olives and thinly sliced red onion.

Wedges of cos or iceberg
with *Blue cheese dressing*

New potato, chicory, smoked salmon
and beetroot salad with *Herbed labne*

Herbed labne

Labne (labneh or labni) is a thickened yogurt made by straining off the whey and is popular throughout the eastern Mediterranean and Middle East, where it is often served as part of a mezze. The straining process increases the fat content, giving labne a more creamy texture. It is often formed into small balls and stored in oil. It is available to buy from larger supermarkets and specialist food stores (you could use thick Greek yogurt in this recipe instead).

125 g/¹⁄₂ cup labne (or strained Greek yogurt)
2 tablespoons extra virgin olive oil
1 tablespoon freshly chopped herbs such as coriander/cilantro, mint and parsley
2 teaspoons freshly squeezed lemon juice
¹⁄₂ teaspoon clear honey
¹⁄₄ teaspoon smoked paprika
salt and freshly ground black pepper

MAKES 200 ML/³⁄₄ CUP

Place all the ingredients in a blender and blend until smooth and creamy. Adjust the seasoning and serve.

Serve the dressing with a new potato, chicory, smoked salmon and beetroot/beet salad.

Creamy Russian

Despite its name, this dressing was invented in the US in the late 19th century and was thought to have originally included caviar, hence the name. Traditionally it was used in a Reuben sandwich, a hot corned beef and sauerkraut sandwich on rye bread. This version is made with sour(ed) cream instead of mayonnaise, but you could substitute mayo (see page 29) if you prefer.

150 ml/²⁄₃ cup sour(ed) cream
1 tablespoon freshly squeezed lemon juice
1 tablespoon hot chilli/chili sauce
1 tablespoon chopped onion
2 teaspoons horseradish sauce
salt and freshly ground black pepper

MAKES 200 ML/³⁄₄ CUP

Place all the ingredients in a bowl and stir well until evenly combined. Adjust the seasoning to taste and serve.

This dressing is perfect served with rare sliced beef, thinly sliced onion and crisp salad leaves.

Avocado and tarragon

Avocado is a superb addition to a creamy salad dressing with its naturally smooth, velvety flesh. It works well with lots of herbs but is particularly good with tarragon and this makes it the perfect dressing for fish- or chicken-based salads - try it as an alterative dressing to a Caesar.

1 small avocado
125 ml/½ cup buttermilk
1 spring onion/scallion,
    finely chopped
2 tablespoons freshly
    chopped tarragon
2 tablespoons avocado oil
1½ tablespoons freshly squeezed
    lemon juice
salt and freshly ground black pepper

MAKES 300 ML/1¼ CUPS

Cut the avocado in half and remove the pit/stone. Scoop the flesh into the food processor and add the buttermilk, spring onion/scallion, tarragon, oil, lemon juice and a little salt and pepper and blend until smooth. Thin with milk or water if necessary, adjust seasoning and serve.

Coconut and chilli

Coconut cream adds a light creaminess to this Asian-inspired dressing.

1 tablespoon peanut oil
125 ml/½ cup coconut cream
1 tablespoon Thai fish sauce
grated zest and freshly squeezed
    juice of ½ lime
1 teaspoon grated root ginger
2 teaspoons honey
1 large red chilli/chile,
    seeded and chopped
a little freshly ground pepper

MAKES 150 ML/⅔ CUP

Whisk all the ingredients together except the chilli/chile, transfer to a bowl and add the chilli/chile. Adjust the seasoning to taste and serve.

This is lovely served with char-grilled scallops, as well as on a chicken and shredded vegetable salad.

Louis

Traditionally served with crab, this creamy, tangy mayonnaise-based dressing was first invented in San Francisco, California in the early 1900s with two hotels laying claim to the recipe.

150 g/²/₃ cup mayonnaise (see page 29)
2 teaspoons mild chilli/chile sauce
1 spring onion/scallion, finely chopped
1 tablespoon pitted/stoned green olives, finely chopped
grated zest and freshly squeezed juice of ¹/₂ lemon
1 teaspoon Worcestershire sauce
1 teaspoon horseradish sauce
salt and freshly ground black pepper

MAKES 250 ML/1 CUP PLUS 1 TABLESPOON

Place all the ingredients in a bowl and whisk together until combined, adjust the seasoning to taste and serve.

Serve with a salad of lettuce, tomatoes, celery, hard-boiled eggs and top with fresh crabmeat.

Marie rose

Marie rose - that archetypical 1970s prawn cocktail dressing - in fact originates from the 1960s and was (most likely) adapted from a far older recipe, Thousand Island dressing. Its ingredients centre around mayonnaise flavoured with tomato ketchup, Worcestershire sauce, lemon juice and pepper but variations can include Tabasco and orange juice amongst other ingredients.

100 g/¹/₂ cup mayonnaise (see page 29)
2 tablespoons tomato ketchup
1 teaspoon Worcestershire sauce
a squeeze of fresh lemon juice
ground white pepper

MAKES 150 ML/²/₃ CUP

Blend all the ingredients together and serve.

Perfect drizzled over prawns/shrimp.

Lettuce, tomatoes, celery and hard-boiled eggs topped with fresh crabmeat with *Louis dressing*

HERBED DRESSINGS

Coriander and herbed toasted sesame • Dill and orange with walnut oil •
Greek oregano • Parsley and green olive • Chive and shallot •
Dill and horseradish • Mexican lime, coriander and chipotle chilli •
Mint salsa verde

Coriander and herbed toasted sesame

The toasted sesame seeds add a wonderfully nutty, smoky flavour to this Japanese-style dressing. It is delicious tossed through a mixed noodle and vegetable salad with avocado and tomatoes. If making ahead, make sure to give it a really good shake before using. This dressing is similar to the traditional Japanese dressing served over wilted spinach.

2 tablespoons sesame seeds
2 large spring onions/scallions, trimmed and chopped
1 tablespoon coriander/cilantro leaves
1 teaspoon caster/granulated sugar
1 tablespoon rice wine vinegar
1 tablespoon light soy sauce
3 tablespoons sunflower oil
2 teaspoons sesame oil
salt and freshly ground black pepper

MAKES 150 ML/²/₃ CUP

Dry fry the sesame seeds in a small frying pan/skillet over a medium heat until toasted and starting to release their aroma. Cool and transfer to a blender. Blend to a paste with the spring onions/scallions, coriander/cilantro, sugar, vinegar, soy sauce and a pinch of salt.

Add both the oils and blend again until amalgamated. Adjust the seasoning and serve.

Dill and orange with walnut oil

The combination of orange, dill and walnut oil is delicious and makes a wonderful dressing for smoked fish salads. You can vary the oil and use hazelnut or extra virgin if preferred.

grated zest and freshly squeezed juice of 1 orange
1 small shallot, finely chopped
1 small garlic clove, crushed
1 tablespoon red wine vinegar
4 tablespoons walnut oil
1 tablespoon freshly chopped dill
salt and freshly ground black pepper

MAKES 150 ML/²/₃ CUP

Place the orange zest and juice, shallot, garlic, vinegar and salt and pepper in a bowl and whisk together. Gradually whisk in the oil until the dressing is amalgamated. Stir in the dill and serve.

This is delicious paired with smoked fish.

Greek oregano

The beauty of travelling is discovering the tastes and flavours of other countries' cuisines and Greece will forever be about simple everyday ingredients transformed by the sun - big juicy tomatoes and sweet sliced onions topped with brilliant white feta and a scattering of dried 'rigani'. Greek oregano in full bloom reaches almost half a metre in height and has small white flowers. It is cut and dried in long stalks, often with the flowers still attached, and it is universally considered the king of oregano. You can buy packets of 'rigani' in specialist food stores.

6 tablespoons Kalamata olive oil
1 tablespoon red wine vinegar
2 teaspoons rigani or dried oregano
salt and freshly ground black pepper

MAKES 75 ML/⅓ CUP

Place all the ingredients in a screw-top jar and shake well until amalgamated. Allow to rest for 30 minutes for the oregano to soften. Shake again and serve.

Serve with a classic Greek salad of tomatoes, onion, green or black olives and feta.

Parsley and green olive

This dressing is similar to a salsa verde or green sauce. It is a vibrant green colour and is great stirred through a pasta, tuna and tomato salad.

3 tablespoons chopped parsley
10 pitted/stoned green olives, roughly chopped
½ shallot, chopped
1 small garlic clove, crushed
1 tablespoon white wine vinegar
125 ml/½ cup extra virgin olive oil
1 tablespoon hot water
salt and freshly ground black pepper

MAKES 125 ML/½ CUP

Place the parsley, olives, shallot, garlic, vinegar and a little salt and pepper in a blender and purée until fairly well chopped. Add the oil and water and blend again until you have a vibrant green sauce. Adjust the seasoning and serve.

Greek salad with
Greek oregano dressing

Chive and shallot

Avocado oil has the most gorgeous deep green luminosity to it, making this a really striking looking dressing. The flavour of avocado oil, however, is milder than extra virgin olive oil and works really well with the shallot and chives in this dressing.

1 shallot, very finely chopped
1 tablespoon freshly chopped chives
1 small garlic clove, crushed
6 tablespoons avocado oil
1 tablespoon freshly squeezed
    lemon juice
a good pinch of caster/
    granulated sugar
salt and freshly ground black pepper

MAKES 125 ML/½ CUP

Place all the ingredients in a screw-top jar, seal the lid and shake well until the dressing is amalgamated. Adjust the seasoning and serve.

Serve this dressing with a crisp bacon and cos/Romaine lettuce salad with garlic croutons.

Dill and horseradish

Use fresh horseradish if you can as the flavour and texture of the root are superior to that found pre-grated in jars – until grated, the root itself has little aroma but as soon as the flesh is damaged the enzymes break down to produce a mustard oil. The grated flesh must be used immediately.

2–3-cm/1-inch piece of horseradish root, peeled (or 2 teaspoons grated horseradish)
1 tablespoon sour(ed) cream
1 tablespoon freshly squeezed lemon juice
1 tablespoon freshly chopped dill
5 tablespoons extra virgin olive oil
salt and freshly ground black pepper

MAKES 200 ML/¾ CUP

If using horseradish root, finely grate the flesh into a bowl (or simply spoon in the pre-grated) and stir in the sour(ed) cream, lemon juice, dill and a little salt and pepper. Then whisk in the oil until the dressing is thickened and smooth. Adjust the seasoning and serve.

This dressing is delicious with a smoked fish and beetroot/beet salad.

Mexican lime, coriander and chipotle chilli

Chipotle chillies/chiles have a smoky flavour and aroma, giving this dressing a lovely rich quality. You can use dried ones if you prefer, but the paste is perfect for dressings. Agave syrup and pumpkin seed oil, once a novelty, are now widely available.

1/2 teaspoon dried chipotle chilli/chile paste
grated zest and freshly squeezed juice of 1 lime
1 teaspoon agave syrup
3 tablespoons pumpkin seed oil
1 tablespoon freshly chopped coriander/cilantro
salt and freshly ground black pepper

MAKES 75 ML/1/3 CUP

Combine the chilli/chile paste, lime zest and juice, agave syrup and a little salt and pepper in a bowl and whisk until smooth. Gradually whisk in the pumpkin seed oil until smooth, then stir in the coriander/cilantro and serve.

Try drizzling over shredded chicken, corn and avocado served on a warmed flour tortilla.

Mint salsa verde

Based on the classic Italian sauce, this lovely dressing is thinned with a little boiling water to give a pouring consistency suitable to dress salads. It is best used straight away whilst the mint remains a bright green colour, but if you want to make it ahead of time, omit the lemon juice and add it just before serving.

1/2 bunch of fresh mint leaves, roughly chopped
1 garlic clove, crushed
1 tablespoon drained capers
2 pitted/stoned green olives, chopped
2 teaspoons freshly squeezed lemon juice
1/2 teaspoon caster/granulated sugar
5 tablespoons extra virgin olive oil
1 tablespoon boiling water
salt and freshly ground black pepper

MAKES 125 ML/1/2 CUP

Place the mint leaves, garlic, capers, olives, lemon juice, sugar, salt and pepper in a blender and whizz until as finely chopped as possible.

Add the oil and water and blend again until you have an evenly blended, vibrant green dressing. Adjust the seasoning to taste.

This is fabulous poured over a char-grilled lamb salad with haricot beans, steamed potatoes and rocket/arugula leaves.

Shredded chicken, corn
and avocado on a tortilla with *Mexican
lime, coriander and chipotle chilli dressing*

FRUITY DRESSINGS

Pink grapefruit and peppercorn • Three citrus • Key West mango and lime • Maple syrup, apple and walnut • Preserved lemon • Homemade pomegranate syrup • Raspberry, mustard and honey • Peach salsa

Pink grapefruit and peppercorn

This dressing is a pretty pale pink colour speckled with the deeper rosy hues of the crushed pink peppercorns. It has a lovely sweet yet slightly bitter note from the grapefruit juice. Pink peppercorns are not actually the same as black pepper but were named so due to their strong resemblance and peppery flavour.

freshly squeezed juice of 1/2 ruby grapefruit, about 3 tablespoons
1/2 teaspoon pink peppercorns, freshly crushed
1 teaspoon caster/granulated sugar
1/2 teaspoon Dijon mustard
4 tablespoons extra virgin olive oil
1 tablespoon freshly chopped chervil, optional
salt

MAKES 125–150 ML/1/2–2/3 CUP

Place the grapefruit juice, pink peppercorns, sugar, mustard and a little salt in a bowl and whisk well, then gradually whisk in the oil until amalgamated. Add the chervil, if using. Adjust the seasoning and serve.

Grapefruit works really well with strong-flavoured fish such as mackerel and would make the perfect dressing for a smoked mackerel, chicory/Belgian endive and grapefruit salad.

Three citrus

Combining three different citrus fruits in the one dressing is inspired and the addition of the grated zest deepens the intensity of the citrus flavour. You can either make your own lemon-flavoured oil (see page 65) or buy one from a specialist food store. Alternatively, this dressing is also good with a plain extra virgin olive oil.

grated zest and freshly squeezed juice of 1/2 lemon
grated zest and freshly squeezed juice of 1/2 lime
grated zest and freshly squeezed juice of 1/2 orange
1 teaspoon whole grain mustard
1–2 teaspoons soft brown sugar
5 tablespoons lemon-infused oil
salt and freshly ground black pepper

MAKES 150 ML/2/3 CUP

Scrub the fruit well before grating the zest into a bowl. Add the juice of all three fruits and stir in the mustard, sugar and salt and pepper until the sugar is dissolved. Whisk in the oil until combined, adjust the seasoning and serve.

This dressing is fabulous drizzled over a shaved fennel, lobster or prawn/shrimp and chervil salad with a few segments of orange.

Key West mango and lime

Mango flesh provides a great base for this pretty dressing, but you will need to buy a ripe mango.

1 small ripe mango, peeled, pitted/stoned and diced
grated zest and freshly squeezed juice of 2 small limes
2 teaspoons clear honey
3 tablespoons avocado oil
1 red chilli/chile, seeded and finely chopped
salt and freshly ground black pepper

MAKES 150 ML/⅔ CUP

Place the mango in a liquidiser with the lime zest, juice, honey and a little salt and pepper and blend until smooth, add the oil and blend again. Transfer to a bowl and stir in the chilli/chile. Adjust the seasoning and serve.

This is a fantastic alternative dressing for a prawn/shrimp cocktail and looks really pretty.

Maple syrup, apple and walnut

This lovely fruity, nutty dressing with a caramel flavour imparted from the maple syrup is very versatile, working well with all types of leaf salads, as well as creamy goat's cheese, Parmesan or other types of cheese. Walnut vinegar is a relatively recent addition to the wide variety of commercial vinegars. If unavailable, cider vinegar is a good alternative.

2 tablespoons clear apple juice
1 tablespoon walnut vinegar or cider vinegar
2 teaspoons maple syrup
1 teaspoon whole grain mustard
3 tablespoons walnut oil
1 tablespoon extra virgin olive oil
salt and freshly ground black pepper

MAKES 100 ML/⅓ CUP PLUS 1 TABLESPOON

Place the apple juice, vinegar, maple syrup and mustard in a bowl with a little salt and pepper and whisk together until smooth. Then gradually whisk in the two oils until emulsified. Adjust the seasoning to taste and serve.

Try crumbling goat's cheese over rocket/arugula leaves and topping with thinly sliced apple, toasted walnuts, shaved Parmesan and a good drizzle of this dressing.

Prawn cocktail with
Key West mango and lime dressing

Preserved lemon

This salty/sour dressing with a hint of sweetness is a real winner and is fantastic served with a crisp green leaf salad or stirred through any couscous salad. Preserved lemons are now quite readily available and can be found in larger supermarkets; alternatively, try Middle Eastern food stores and delis.

4 tablespoons extra virgin olive oil
1 tablespoon preserved lemon, diced
1 garlic clove, crushed
1 tablespoon freshly squeezed lemon juice
2 teaspoon clear honey
1 tablespoon freshly chopped coriander/cilantro
salt and freshly ground black pepper

MAKES 150 ML/²/₃ CUP

Combine all the ingredients in a blender and blend until smooth and vibrant green.

Drizzle over a salad of couscous, shredded grilled chicken, tomatoes and fresh spring onions/scallions.

Homemade pomegranate syrup

This lovely syrup is the most stunning deep pink colour and has a wonderfully fruity flavour. It is a great addition to a salad dressing and can be stored for up to a week in the fridge. It can also simply be lightly drizzled over dishes, as well as frozen yogurt for a sweet treat.

175 ml/³⁄₄ cup fresh pomegranate juice (2 large pomegranates)
125 g/²⁄₃ cup caster/granulated sugar
1 tablespoon freshly squeezed lemon juice
1 teaspoon Dijon mustard
5 tablespoons extra virgin olive oil
salt and freshly ground black pepper

MAKES 125 ML/½ CUP

To make the juice, lightly bash the pomegranates on a board then cut in half, holding them over a bowl to catch the juices. Scoop out all the seeds and flesh into the bowl and pass through a sieve/strainer – you should have about 175 ml /³⁄₄ cup of juice.

Place the pomegranate juice and sugar in a small saucepan and heat gently, stirring until the sugar is dissolved. Increase the heat and simmer for 15 minutes until the juice is syrup-like and reduced to about 125 ml/½ cup. Set aside to cool completely.

Combine 2 tablespoons of the cooled syrup with the lemon juice, mustard and a little salt and pepper and gradually whisk in the oil until emulsified. Adjust the seasoning to taste.

This lovely dressing is great served with a Parma ham and melon salad or any combination of cured meat and fruit.

Raspberry, mustard and honey

The combination of sweet flavours with savoury ones works so well in fruit-based dressings. When fresh raspberries are out of season or unavailable you can easily use frozen strawberries, thawed.

100 g/2/3 cup fresh raspberries
1 tablespoon red wine vinegar
1 tablespoon clear honey
2 teaspoons whole grain mustard
3 tablespoons extra virgin olive oil
salt and freshly ground black pepper

MAKES 175 ML/3/4 CUP

Place the raspberries, vinegar, honey, mustard and a little salt and pepper in a blender and whizz until smooth. Transfer to a bowl and whisk in the two oils until evenly blended. Adjust the seasoning to taste.

Serve with a smoked duck or smoked chicken and leaf salad.

Peach salsa

The pairing of fruit and vanilla with a savoury dish is always a winner. Here white flesh peaches have been used, but you could use pitted/stoned cherries, raspberries or strawberries to great effect.

1 small shallot, finely chopped
seeds from 1/2 vanilla pod/bean
freshly squeezed juice of 1/2 orange
2 teaspoons sherry vinegar
5 tablespoons extra virgin olive oil
1 ripe white flesh peach, pitted/stoned and diced
1 tablespoon freshly chopped mint
salt and freshly ground black pepper

MAKES 275 ML/1 CUP PLUS 2 TABLESPOONS

Whisk together the shallot, vanilla seeds, orange juice and vinegar and then gradually whisk in the oil until amalgamated. Stir in the peach and fresh mint and season to taste with salt and pepper.

Serve this dressing over a salad of duck breast, mixed leaves and fine green beans.

duck breast, mixed leaves and
fine green beans with *Peach salsa*

INFUSED DRESSINGS

Lemon, olive and pepper oil • Bay and thyme oil • Smoked garlic oil •
Saffron oil • Chilli oil • Garlic oil • Piri-piri • Basil oil

Lemon, olive and pepper oil

The oil is infused with lemon zest and slices, crushed olives and peppercorns for a few days, allowing the flavours to permeate the oil. The oil is then strained, ready for vinegar or lemon juice to be added.

1 lemon
8 large pitted/stoned green olives, sliced
1/2 teaspoon each black and pink peppercorns, bruised
150 ml/2/3 cup extra virgin olive oil
freshly squeezed lemon juice, to taste
salt

MAKES 150 ML/2/3 CUP

Thinly pare the zest from the lemon and then using a sharp knife cut away the pith from the whole lemon. Cut the lemon into thin slices. Place zest and slices in a sterilized jar (see page 4) with the olives, and peppercorns (bashed slightly). Pour over the oil and leave to infuse for 5 days.

Strain off and discard the flavourings and pour the oil into a bowl. Whisk in enough lemon juice for your taste and adjust the seasoning.

This is lovely drizzled over tomatoes, and is also good with a tuna and white bean salad.

Bay and thyme oil

Bay and thyme give this oil a lovely mellow flavour and once strained it is perfectly enhanced with a light vinegar such as Chinese black vinegar or rice wine vinegar.

6 bay leaves
4 sprigs of fresh thyme
150 ml/2/3 cup extra virgin olive oil
1–2 tablespoons of vinegar of your choice
salt and freshly ground black pepper

MAKES 200 ML/3/4 CUP

Place the bay leaves, thyme, salt and pepper in a pestle and mortar and pound gently to bash up the herbs. Transfer to a sterilized jar (see page 4), add the oil and marinate for 5 days.

Strain the oil into a jar, add the vinegar, salt and pepper to taste and serve.

This dressing is great served over any salad leaves, or shaved courgettes/zucchini.

Smoked garlic oil

Tea-smoking is a terrific way to flavour foods with a rich and intense smoke flavour. It is often used to smoke salmon or duck but works well here with the garlic. You will need to double line the wok with foil and it's a good idea to open a window when you are smoking foods as the aroma is quite pungent.

8 tablespoons soft brown sugar
8 tablespoons long grain rice
8 tablespoons tea leaves
1 head of garlic
250 ml/1 cup plus 1 tablespoon
    extra virgin olive oil
vinegar or freshly squeezed
    lemon juice, to taste
salt and freshly ground black pepper

MAKES 300 ML/1¼ CUPS

Line a wok with a double sheet of foil and combine the brown sugar, rice and tea leaves in the bottom. Place a small rack or griddle over the smoking mixture (making sure they don't touch) and lay the garlic on the rack.

Place the wok over a high heat and as soon as the mixture starts to smoke, cover the wok with a tightly fitting lid. Lower the heat and cook gently for 15 minutes until the garlic turns a deep brown. Allow to cool.

Place the unpeeled garlic in a sterilized bottle or jar (see page 4), add the oil and allow to infuse for 1 week. Drain and use the oil to make a dressing, adding vinegar or lemon juice to taste.

Great with a beef carpaccio or a char-grilled lamb salad.

Saffron oil

The saffron adds both a pretty colour and a lovely delicate flavour to this oil, which is delicious when drizzled over a mixed leaf and tomato salad.

a large pinch of saffron strands
1 tablespoon water
1 tablespoon white wine vinegar
1 teaspoon caster/granulated sugar
4 tablespoons extra virgin olive oil
salt and freshly ground black pepper

MAKES 100 ML/⅓ CUP PLUS 1 TABLESPOON

Place the saffron, water, vinegar and sugar in a small saucepan and heat gently, stirring until the sugar is dissolved. Bring to the boil and remove from the heat. Set aside to cool completely.

Add the oil, season to taste and serve.

Chilli oil

Chilli/chile oil is a great addition to any store cupboard. Once strained, the oil will keep in the fridge for a month but be sure to return to room temperature before use.

30 g/6 whole dried chillies/chiles
250 ml/1 cup peanut oil

MAKES 250 ML/1 CUP

Put the chillies/chiles in a bowl, cover with hot water and leave to soak for 30 minutes until slightly softened. Drain well and discard the soaking water. Put the softened chillies/chiles in a food processor and blend to a rough paste.

Transfer the paste to a small saucepan, pour in the oil and set over a medium heat to warm gently, until the mixtures comes the boil. Boil for 1 minute, then remove the pan from the heat and leave to cool completely.

Strain the oil through a fine mesh sieve/strainer, pour into a sterilized jar (see page 4) and seal. Keep in the fridge for up to 1 month and use as required.

Garlic oil

This oil is particularly good drizzled over noodle salads but as it doesn't keep as well as chilli/chile oil, so make it in smaller quantities, store in the fridge and use it up within two weeks.

1 whole head of garlic
125 ml/½ cup peanut oil

MAKES 125 ML/½ CUP

Peel each garlic clove and cut into slices 3 mm/⅛ in. thick.

Put the peanut oil in a small saucepan and set over a low heat until shimmering. Add the garlic slices and cook for about 20 minutes until they are crisp and golden but not burnt.

Remove the garlic with a slotted spoon and drain on paper towels. Reserve the oil, straining several times through a fine mesh sieve/strainer to discard any small bits of garlic and set aside to cool completely. Pour into a sterilized jar (see page 4) and seal. Keep in the fridge for up to 2 weeks and use as required.

The garlic slices can be used in salads or as a soup topping, but will only keep for a few days in the fridge.

Char-grilled chicken
with *Piri piri dressing*

Piri-piri

This is a classic Portuguese dressing traditionally drizzled over char-grilled chicken. Despite the fact that this recipe uses only 8 small dried red chillies/chiles (traditionally African bird's eye chillies/chiles are used in Portugal), it packs a powerful punch. Italian dried pepperoncino chillies/chiles work well, too.

8 small dried red chillies/chiles
250 ml/1 cup plus 1 tablespoon extra virgin olive oil
2 garlic cloves, crushed
grated zest of 1 lemon
2 tablespoons white wine vinegar
salt and freshly ground black pepper

MAKES 300 ML/1¼ CUPS

Finely chop the chillies/chiles and place in a sterilized jar (see page 4), top up with the oil and leave to infuse for 1–2 weeks. Add the garlic, lemon zest, vinegar and a little salt and pepper, shake well and serve.

As well as grilled chicken, this dressing is also fabulous over char-grilled calamari/squid, prawns/shrimp and fresh sardines.

Basil oil

This dressing is not only a beautiful colour but is also really fragrant with pungent fresh basil leaves. It is best made in the summer months when basil is at its prime, and of course most inexpensive.

25 g/³⁄₄ oz. fresh basil leaves
300 ml/1¼ cups extra virgin olive oil
a little freshly squeezed lemon juice
a pinch of salt

MAKES 300 ML/1¼ CUPS

Blitz the basil leaves, oil and a little salt in a food processor or liquidiser to make a vivid green paste. Infuse overnight and the next day strain the oil through a layer of muslin/cheesecloth into a sterilized jar (see page 4). Store the oil in the fridge, returning to room temperature before use.

This dressing is best served with lemon juice but rather than mixing the juice into the oil add it directly to the salad.

Arrange a plate of heirloom tomatoes and drizzle over some basil oil, squeeze with a little lemon juice and serve.

WARM DRESSINGS

Greek island • Onion and Moroccan spice • Mirin •
Black bean and ginger • Sherry, orange and raisin •
Lemon, honey and shallot • Caramelized garlic • Smoked chilli

Greek island

With flavours reminiscent of travels to the Greek islands, this dressing is delicious drizzled over a grilled lamb salad with white beans, char-grilled/broiled courgettes/zucchini and black olives.

6 tablespoons extra virgin olive oil
1/2 red onion, finely chopped
1 garlic clove, crushed
grated zest and freshly squeezed juice of 1/2 lemon
a pinch of dried chilli/hot red pepper flakes
2 teaspoons freshly chopped rosemary
1 teaspoon freshly chopped thyme
1 small tomato, peeled, seeded and diced
salt and freshly ground black pepper

MAKES 150 ML/2/3 CUP

Heat 2 tablespoons of the oil in a frying pan/skillet and gently fry the onion, garlic, lemon zest, chilli/hot red pepper flakes and herbs with a little salt and pepper for 5 minutes until softened.

Stir in the lemon juice and then whisk in the remaining oil. Remove the pan from the heat, stir in the tomato and adjust the seasoning to taste. Serve at once.

Onion and Moroccan spice

This is a super dressing for a chickpea salad with shredded chicken, raisins, tomatoes, toasted almonds and chopped fresh herbs. The pomegranate syrup used here is the recipe from page 59 (or, if you like a more tart flavour, you could use pomegranate molasses with 1/2 teaspoon honey).

5 tablespoons extra virgin olive oil
1/2 small onion, thinly sliced
1 garlic clove, crushed
1 teaspoon Moroccan spice mix
2 teaspoons homemade pomegranate syrup (see page 59)
1 tablespoon finely sliced preserved lemon
1 tablespoon red wine vinegar
salt and freshly ground black pepper

MAKES 150 ML/2/3 CUP

Heat 2 tablespoons of the oil in a small frying pan/skillet and gently fry the onion, garlic, spice mix and a little salt and pepper over a low heat for 5 minutes. Stir in the pomegranate syrup and warm through.

Remove the pan from the heat and whisk in the remaining oil. Stir in the preserved lemon and vinegar and adjust the seasoning taste. Serve at once.

Mirin

This is a mildly flavoured Japanese-style dressing with a little sweetness from the mirin, balanced beautifully with the rice wine vinegar. It is lovely served warm poured over oysters on the half shell or even seared scallops.

50 ml/3½ tablespoons mirin
1 spring onion/scallion, trimmed and thinly sliced
1 garlic clove, sliced
2 tablespoons rice wine vinegar
1 tablespoon dark soy sauce
2 tablespoons peanut or sunflower oil
1 tablespoon freshly chopped coriander/cilantro

MAKES 150 ML/²/₃ CUP

Place the mirin, half the spring onion/scallion, the garlic, vinegar and soy sauce in a small pan. Bring to the boil and simmer gently for 2 minutes. Strain the liquid through a sieve/strainer and set aside to cool to slightly.

Whisk in the oil, stir in the coriander/cilantro and remaining spring onion/scallion and serve at once.

Black bean and ginger

This pungent dressing really packs a punch with the salty beans, ginger and chilli/chile. Salted black beans are available either vacuum packed or in cans from Asian food stores.

2 tablespoons salted black beans
3 tablespoons sunflower oil
1 large red chilli/chile, seeded and chopped
1 garlic clove, thinly sliced
1 teaspoon grated root ginger
1 tablespoon black vinegar or rice wine vinegar
3 tablespoons Chinese rice wine
2 teaspoons light soy sauce
1 teaspoon clear honey

MAKES 200 ML/¾ CUP

Soak the salted beans in cold water for 30 minutes, drain well and pat dry with paper towels.

Heat the oil in a small frying pan/skillet and gently fry the chilli/chile, garlic and ginger over a low heat for 3–4 minutes until softened. Add the black beans, vinegar, Chinese rice wine and soy sauce and warm through. Stir in the honey.

Serve at once drizzled over a charred pork, noodle and sugar snap pea salad.

Charred pork, noodle and sugar snap peas
with *Black bean and ginger dressing*

Sherry, orange and raisin

Pedro Ximenez is an intensely sweet dessert sherry made from grapes grown in various regions throughout Spain. In South America it is known as Pedro Gimenez. If unavailable, you could use Masala or an alcohol-free alternative such as raisin juice.

2 tablespoons extra virgin olive oil
30 g/1 oz. blanched whole hazelnuts
30 g/1 oz. sultanas/golden raisins
3 tablespoons Pedro Ximenez, sweet sherry
    or raisin juice
2 tablespoons sherry vinegar
grated zest and freshly squeezed juice of 1 orange
    (about 50 ml/3½ tablespoons)
4 tablespoons hazelnut oil
salt and freshly ground black pepper

MAKES 200 ML/¾ CUP

Heat the olive oil in a frying pan/skillet and gently fry the hazelnuts for 1–2 minutes until golden, add the raisins and fry for a further 1 minute until soft.

Add the sherry and sherry vinegar to the pan and bubble for 30 seconds. Whisk in the orange zest and juice and warm through, then remove from the heat and transfer to a bowl.

Gradually whisk in the hazelnut oil and season to taste. Serve at once.

Perfect with a salad of duck, chicory/Belgian endive and orange segments.

Lemon, honey and shallot

The zing of lemon balanced with sweet honey combines to make a delicious dressing. Warm dressings are ideally suited to serving with cooked meat and fish-based salads and this one is especially good drizzled over char-grilled chicken with a mixed green salad.

6 tablespoons extra virgin olive oil
grated zest and freshly squeezed juice
    of 1 large lemon
1 garlic clove, crushed
1 small shallot, finely diced
1 large red chilli/chile, seeded and finely chopped
1 teaspoon cumin seeds, bashed
2 teaspoons clear honey
salt and freshly ground black pepper

MAKES 250 ML/1 CUP

Heat half the oil in a frying pan/skillet and gently fry the lemon zest, garlic, shallot, chilli/chile, cumin seeds and a little salt and pepper over a very low heat for 2–3 minutes until soft but not golden.

Add the lemon juice and honey and stir well. Remove the pan from the heat and pour into a bowl. Whisk in the remaining oil, season to taste and serve at once.

Caramelized garlic

The garlic is braised in olive oil until softened, resulting in a sweet garlic paste. This is then blended with the remaining ingredients, making a lovely creamy dressing. It needs to be used immediately as once it sits it will separate.

1 head of garlic
125 ml/½ cup extra virgin olive oil
2 tablespoons white wine vinegar
salt and freshly ground black pepper

MAKES 200 ML/¾ CUP

Peel the garlic cloves, place them in a small saucepan and cover with the oil. Heat gently and cook over a low heat for 20 minutes until the garlic has really softened.

Strain the oil into a jug/pitcher. Transfer the garlic to a blender, add the vinegar, salt and pepper and blend until smooth. Gradually whisk in the oil until the dressing is emulsified.

This can be used as an alternative to a Caesar dressing, drizzled over mixed leaves, croutons and with crispy fried bacon replacing the anchovies.

Smoked chilli

Ancho chilli/chile is the name given to a poblano chilli/chile when it's dried and means 'wide' in Spanish, as it becomes flat and wide as it dries. It has a mellow sweet aroma, giving this dressing a distinctive flavour and deep red colour.

1 dried ancho chilli/chile
300 ml/1¼ cups boiling water
2 tablespoons sunflower oil
1 spring onion/scallion, finely sliced
1 garlic clove, crushed
grated zest and freshly squeezed juice of 1 lime
2 teaspoons agave syrup
2 tablespoons pumpkin seed oil
salt and freshly ground black pepper

MAKES 150 ML/⅔ CUP

Place the chilli/chile in a bowl, cover with the boiling water and allow to soak for 15 minutes until softened. Cut in half and discard seeds and stalk. Finely chop the flesh and set aside.

Heat the sunflower oil in a small frying pan/skillet and gently fry the spring onion/scallion and garlic for 3 minutes until softened. Add the chilli/chile, lime zest and juice and agave syrup and warm through. Remove the pan from the heat, stir in the pumpkin oil until evenly blended and season to taste.

Serve at once drizzled over a grilled corn.

Mixed leaves and fried croutons
with *Caramelized garlic dressing*

SIMPLE SALADS

Simple leaf and herb salad • Summer vegetable carpaccio • Red chicory,
roquefort and hazelnut salad • Grilled asparagus and goat's cheese salad •
Chickpea, egg and potato salad • Black bean salad with avocado and lime •
Crab and artichoke salad • Lobster and fennel salad • Fragrant herb couscous salad •
Aubergine and pomegranate salad • Orange and red onion salad •
Pea shoot and crispy noodle salad

Simple leaf and herb salad

There are thousands of recipes for simple leaf salads, but incorporating a delicious mixture of fresh herbs ensures a version that will always impress. Finish with your choice of classic vinaigrette.

inner leaves from 2 large cos/Romaine lettuces
250 g/8 oz. mixed salad leaves, such as radicchio, mâche, mizuna or chicory/Belgian endive
a handful of mixed, fresh soft-leaf herbs such as basil, chives, dill and mint
Mustard Vinaigrette (see page 25) or French Vinaigrette (see page 24), to dress

SERVES 4

First make the vinaigrette and set aside.

Wash the leaves, spin dry in a salad spinner (or pat dry with paper towels) and transfer to a plastic bag. Chill for 30 minutes to make the leaves crisp. Put the leaves and herbs into a large salad bowl, add a little of the vinaigrette and toss well to coat evenly. Add a little more to taste, then serve at once.

Summer vegetable carpaccio

In this refreshing carpaccio, the nearly transparent slices of vegetable are enhanced with your choice of tangy sour-sweet Asian dressing. You can use any firm vegetable - the key is to slice them paper-thin so that they can absorb the dressing and tenderize. Using a mandoline-type slicer will ensure neat, thin shaving. It makes a lovely light appetizer or side dish and is just right for summer eating.

5 large radishes
1/2 a fennel bulb
1 large courgette/zucchini
1/2 a red onion
Chilli and Sesame Dressing (see page 18) or Japanese-style Sweet Miso and Sesame Dressing (see page 14), to dress

SERVES 4-6

First make the dressing and set aside.

Using a mandoline, vegetable peeler or very sharp knife, carefully slice the radishes, fennel, courgette/zucchini and red onion as finely as possibly. Put the prepared vegetables in a bowl.

To assemble, pour the dressing over the prepared vegetables and toss well to coat evenly. Use salad servers to arrange the salad on serving plates and serve at once.

Red chicory, roquefort and hazelnut salad

This simple salad provides a delicious contrast of textures between the crunchy nuts, crisp leaves and creamy blue cheese. A simple dressing made with hazelnut oil and raspberry vinegar finishes it to perfection. Enjoy as a light meal or appetizer.

50 g/⅓ cup roasted, skinned hazelnuts*
2 heads of red or green chicory/Belgian endive
2 Comice or Conference pears, peeled, cored
    and cut into 8 segments
100 g/¾ cup Roquefort, roughly crumbled
Hazelnut Vinaigrette (see page 22), to dress

SERVES 4

First make the vinaigrette and set aside.

Preheat the oven to 160°C fan/180°C/350°F/ Gas 4. Freshen up the hazelnuts by roasting them in the oven or toasting them in a dry frying pan/skillet. Set aside to cool, then chop roughly.

Separate out the chicory/Belgian endive leaves and place in a bowl of iced water for 15–20 minutes. Drain and pat the leaves dry with paper towels. Arrange the salad on plates starting with a pile of leaves, then the pear segments and Roquefort. Spoon the vinaigrette over the salad, top with the chopped hazelnuts and serve at once.

*If you can't find skinned hazelnuts, roast them with their skins on until dark brown then rub off the skins with a kitchen towel.

Grilled asparagus and goat's cheese salad

Simple and delicious, this recipe will serve 4 as an appetizer or 2 as a main course salad. Use a creamy goat's cheese with a rind that will soften nicely without melting.

450 g/1 lb. fresh asparagus spears
1 tablespoon Bay and Thyme Oil (see page 65), plus extra
    to dress (you will need to infuse the oil 5 days in advance)
120 g/4 oz. goat's cheese, sliced
sea salt and freshly ground black pepper
crusty bread, to serve

SERVES 2–4

Preheat the grill/broiler. Trim the asparagus spears and rub or brush with a little of the bay and thyme oil, sprinkle with salt and pepper, and cook under the hot grill/broiler for 4–5 minutes, turning half-way through until charred and tender.

Arrange on plates and top each one with a slice of the cheese, return to the grill/broiler very briefly until the cheese is softened but not browned. Sprinkle with more oil and serve with crusty bread.

Chickpea, egg and potato salad

A pleasing combination of flavours and textures, the nutty chickpeas are bound together by the slightly broken-up potato, hard-boiled/cooked egg and oily dressing. It tastes best when it's still warm.

250 g/1¼ cups cooked, soaked dried chickpeas, or the contents of 1 x 400-g/14-oz. can, drained
500 g/1 lb. 2 oz. salad potatoes, boiled and bashed gently
3 hard-boiled/cooked eggs, peeled and roughly chopped
a handful of fresh chives, chopped/snipped
3 tablespoons Parsley and Green Olive Dressing (see page 46), plus extra to dress

SERVES 4

First make the dressing and set aside.

Mash one-third of the chickpeas slightly, then mix them with the whole chickpeas and the potatoes. Add 3 tablespoons of the dressing and stir well.

Distribute the chopped eggs through the salad, taking care not to break them up too much. Drizzle with a little more dressing, sprinkle the chives over the surface and serve at once.

Black bean salad with avocado and lime

The Aztecs were already eating guacamole at the time of the Spanish Conquest, and the winning combination of avocado, chilli/chile, tomato and coriander/cilantro leaves, laced with lime, is now universally popular. Here, by chopping the avocado instead of mashing it, and stirring in some cooked black beans, you have a salad with a distinctly Mexican flavour which is equally irresistible.

1 x 400-g/ 14-oz. can black beans, rinsed and drained
2 ripe avocados, stoned/pitted, peeled and chopped
250 g/8 oz. cherry tomatoes, cut in half
2 spring onions/scallions, trimmed and finely chopped
a handful of fresh coriander/cilantro leaves, to garnish
salt and freshly ground black pepper
Mexican Lime, Coriander and Chipotle Chilli Dressing (see page 50), to dress

SERVES 4

First make the dressing and set aside.

Put the beans, avocados, tomatoes and spring onions/scallions into a large salad bowl and pour a few tablespoons of the dressing over. Toss everything together until all of the ingredients are combined, garnish with extra coriander/cilantro leaves and serve at once.

Crab and artichoke salad

Artichoke and crab both have an affinity with tarragon so my simple herbed vinaigrette works perfectly here. Try to use fresh crab meat for the best flavour and texture.

a bunch of rocket/arugula
1 head of radicchio (round or long)
500 g/1 lb. 2 oz. cooked crab meat (see recipe introduction)
6 cherry tomatoes, cut in half
4 artichoke hearts in oil, quartered
a handful of flat-leaf parsley leaves, roughly chopped
sea salt and freshly ground black pepper
2 chunks of country bread, chopped into cubes and toasted
finely grated lemon zest, to garnish
Tarragon Vinaigrette, to dress (see page 11)

SERVES 4

First make the vinaigrette and set aside.

Wash and dry the rocket/arugula and divide between 4 plates. Core the radicchio and then add to the rocket/arugula on the plates.

Add a quarter of the crab meat to each plate. Top with a quarter of the cherry tomatoes, artichokes and parsley.

Scatter over the the croutons and lemon zest, drizzle with the vinaigrette and serve at once.

Lobster and fennel salad

A simple dish with lovely flavours - when you serve lobster, the effect is instantly luxurious and 'special occasion'. Who would ever know this dish was so simple to prepare? Slice the fennel as finely as possible, using a mandoline if you have one.

1 large bulb of fennel
freshly squeezed juice of 1/2 lemon
4 tablespoons/1/4 cup extra virgin olive oil
4 small cooked lobsters, about 500 g/1 lb. 2 oz. each,
    or 2 large ones
4 heaped tablespoons Saffron Alioli (see page 30),
    to serve
sea salt and freshly ground black pepper

SERVES 4

First make the alioli, cover and chill until ready to serve.

Trim off and discard the tough outer layer of fennel, then chop and reserve the fronds. Cut the bulb in half, then cut crossways into very thin slices. Put in a bowl, add the lemon juice, oil, fennel fronds, salt and pepper, toss well, then let marinate for 15 minutes.

Cut the lobsters in half and lift the tail flesh out of the shell. Crack the claws with a small hammer or crab crackers and carefully remove all the meat.

Put a layer of shaved fennel salad on each plate, top with the lobster, and serve at once, topped with a spoonful of saffron alioli.

Fragrant herb couscous salad

Tabbouleh, the fresh parsley salad from Lebanon, is based on bulghur wheat. This one is made with couscous, the fine Moroccan pasta and drizzled with my Preserved Lemon dressing. This is delicious topped with grilled chicken or char-grilled slices of halloumi cheese.

300 g/1¹/₂ cups couscous
freshly squeezed juice of 1 lemon
2 tablespoons chopped fresh basil
2 tablespoons chopped fresh coriander/cilantro
2 tablespoons chopped fresh mint
2 tablespoons chopped fresh flat-leaf parsley
sea salt and freshly ground black pepper
Preserved Lemon Dressing, to dress (see page 58)

SERVES 4

First make the dressing and set aside..

Put the couscous in a bowl, add water to cover by 5 cm/2 inches and let soak for 10 minutes.

Drain the soaked couscous, shaking the sieve/strainer well to remove any excess water. Transfer to a large bowl, add the lemon juice, chopped basil, coriander/cilantro, mint and parsley. Season with salt and pepper, then set aside to let the flavours develop.

Drizzle with the dressing and serve at once.

Aubergine and pomegranate salad

This recipe is so simple and utterly delicious. Salting aubergines/eggplants means they will fry better, absorb less oil and have a superior flavour.

2 medium aubergines/eggplants, cut lengthways into 4-mm/¹/₈-inch thick slices
3 tablespoons olive oil
grated zest and freshly squeezed juice of 2 lemons
2 garlic cloves, finely chopped
1¹/₂ tablespoons white wine vinegar
1¹/₂ tablespoons good-quality extra virgin olive oil
a handful of mint, roughly chopped
a handful of flat-leaf parsley, roughly chopped
1 pomegranate, seeded
100 g/3¹/₂ oz. firm pecorino cheese, shaved
sea salt and freshly ground black pepper
Homemade Pomegranate Syrup, to drizzle (see page 59)

SERVES 4

Sprinkle the aubergine/eggplant slices with salt. Weigh down and leave for 15 minutes. Remove and pat dry with paper towels.

Heat the olive oil in a large, heavy frying pan/skillet and fry the aubergine/eggplant slices. (Choose a ridged pan if you can.)

Mix the lemon zest and juice, garlic, vinegar and oil, then mix this dressing with the aubergine/eggplant slices, and scatter with the chopped herbs, pomegranate seeds and pecorino. Drizzle with pomegranate syrup to taste and serve at once.

Orange and red onion salad

The blood orange is one of the Mediterranean island of Sicily's most famous exports. They are strongly fragrant with brilliant red peel and pulp. This salad is unashamedly simple and also works well with small sweet oranges when blood oranges are out of season.

4 blood oranges or other small sweet oranges
1 small red onion, cut into very thin rings
a handful of flat-leaf parsley leaves, freshly chopped
sea salt and freshly ground black pepper
3–4 tablespoons Dill and Orange Dressing (see page 45), made with extra virgin olive oil

SERVES 4

First make the dressing (using extra virgin olive oil rather than walnut oil) and set aside.

Peel the oranges and remove the pith. Cut horizontally into thin slices and put in a bowl.

Add the onion rings to the bowl with the oranges. Add 3–4 tablespoons of dressing and half of the parsley, season with salt and pepper and toss until all the ingredients are well coated.

Arrange the oranges and onion rings on a serving plate. Drizzle with a little more dressing to taste, sprinkle with the remaining chopped parsley and serve at once.

Pea shoot and crispy noodle salad

Pea shoots are the tendrils and baby leaves of mangetouts/snowpeas. You often see them in Chinese and Southeast Asian markets, but if you can't find any, use watercress instead. It gives a delicious peppery flavour, which mirrors the fiery spice of wasabi, used here in the mayonnaise.

100 g/3½ oz. dried Chinese egg noodles, soaked and drained according to the directions on the package
200 g/7 oz. pea shoots or watercress
125 g/4 oz. radishes, sliced and cut into strips
sea salt
peanut or safflower oil, for deep-frying
Wasabi Mayonnaise, to dress (see page 29)

SERVES 4

First make the mayonaise, cover and chill until ready to serve.

Heat 5 cm/2 inches of oil in deep saucepan to 180°C/350°F on a sugar/candy thermometer (or a cube of bread crisps and browns in 30 seconds). Break the noodles into 5-cm/2-inch lengths and add to the oil in 4 batches (be careful because the fat will foam up as the noodles are added). Fry for 1–2 minutes until crisp. Drain on paper towels and sprinkle with salt.

Put the pea shoots and radishes in a bowl and add a few tablespoons of wasabi mayonnaise. Toss until lightly and evenly coated, top with the crispy noodles and serve at once.

Index

Credits

All photography by Ian Wallace with the exception of images on the following pages: Peter Cassidy 26, 40, 62; Richard Jung 3, 8; Mowie Kay 50, 86; David Munns 90, 93, 94; Steve Painter 1, 27; William Reavell 34, 46, 65, 83, 85, 89; Matt Russell 4, 5, 72, 82; Kate Whitaker 11, 87; Clare Winfield 56, 63, 80.

All text by Louise Pickford with the exception of the following salad recipes: Fiona Beckett 87 l; Ursula Ferrigno 91 l, 92 r & 94 l; Vicky Jones 88 l & r; Chloe Coker & Jane Montgomery 84 r.